THE
PERSONAL
ORACLE

BOOK OF MEANING

THE PERSONAL ORACLE

Book of Meaning

by

Coleman Stevenson

&

Deck & book by Coleman Stevenson

Copyright © 2018 by The Dark Exact, LLC

The Dark Exact, LLC
PO Box 11865
Portland, OR 97211
www.etsy.com/shop/TheDarkExact
www.instagram.com/darkexact/

PERSONALIZING YOUR ORACLE

YOUR PERSONAL ORACLE

This miniature oracle has been designed not just as a divination tool but as a way for users to examine the self more deeply through their connections to each of the thirty-nine images on the cards. The imagery in this deck includes symbols common in "fortune telling" decks from the early the 20th Century, as well as new symbols of importance to me as an artist and person, all illustrated in classic oracle style.

Instead of this booklet providing meanings for the cards, it offers an opportunity for users to explore personal associations and feelings about each symbol before any cards are drawn. The meanings each user assigns to the cards, whether universal, highly personal, or a combination of both, will reveal the inner workings of the mind.

GENERAL INSTRUCTIONS

For each card, record the first ideas that come to mind when viewing the image. Next, spend some time with each one, noting any additional impressions, memories, and associations. Consider both positive and negative aspects of each concept you associate with the oracle images. You may wish to add to your meanings after you've been using the deck for a while. As you change, so will the cards.

A mini-guidebook has also been included with your cards. After you've explored each image, transfer your condensed meanings to its pages and keep it with your deck for a quick reference when reading.

There are no right or wrong answers in this process. Each person viewing the symbols brings a different set of personal and cultural experiences and beliefs, as well as a different eye to the images themselves. Look closely at each image and take your time exploring the details. (I'll cite an interesting example of differences in seeing in the next paragraph, but if you don't want your personal interpretations to be colored by outside suggestions, skip to the following section for now and come back after you've assigned your meanings.)

Example of interpretation details: When this deck was in the early stages and consisted mostly of traditional oracle imagery, a friend of mine and I were discussing the included Anchor card. I am so used to seeing various versions of this card, my eye tended to move quickly from image to idea, but my friend, viewing it freshly, was able to notice certain details I had missed. He focused in on the fact that the rope appears to be cut. In my mind, the anchor was either stability or heaviness, but to him it symbolized being either unmoored or freed.

SUGGESTIONS FOR READING

After you have assigned meanings to all of the images, shuffle the cards face down. As you shuffle, ask the cards a question or think about a situation in your life for which you would like some guidance. For the following simple spread, draw the cards one at a time and place them face up in a row, left to right. The card on the left will tell you something about your past; the card in the middle will indicate something about your present circumstances; the card on the right is a *possible* future event.

```
┌──────┐   ┌──────┐   ┌──────┐
│      │   │      │   │      │
│ PAST │   │PRESENT│  │FUTURE│
│      │   │      │   │      │
└──────┘   └──────┘   └──────┘
```

Use the card meanings you've recorded in this guide to understand more about your situation. They may reveal insights previously overlooked, show you areas for caution, and suggest possible ways to avoid difficulty. These cards do not necessarily predict the future. They are a tool to help you consider new perspectives and possible courses of action.

You can use these cards in any spread for divination and self study. You can also simply draw a single card any time a hint of guidance is needed, or a question needs to be answered.

You might also examine the meanings you have assigned to the cards, looking for patterns that reveal additional information about your tendencies, desires, beliefs, hopes, and fears.

Reading for Others

If you use this deck to perform readings for other people, you have a few options for how to proceed:

1. You can simply accept the values you've assigned to the cards as THE meanings, using the deck as you would any deck that comes with its own preset interpretations.

2. If you feel like the previous approach might be projecting your worldview too forcefully onto others, you can involve them more in the reading process. Invite them to offer their impressions of cards as you draw them from the deck, much the same way as when you were initially working within the pages of this book.

3. You might also discover that a combined approach of these two methods gives the strongest reading.

ADDITIONAL USES

These cards can also be used in creative exercises. Pull cards to serve as prompts or inspiration for writing or making art. For example, you might pull a single card to give yourself a theme for a new piece, or a series of cards to help weave together a new story. If you are experiencing a creative block in an existing project, pull a card or two for advice on how to proceed.

The uses for these cards certainly goes beyond anything described in this booklet. Just like you are adding your own interpretations, add your own processes for using the Personal Oracle. The possibilities are as endless as your imagination.

SHARE YOUR INTERPRETATIONS

Want to share your symbolism or see what others are assigning to their cards? Use the hashtag #personaloracle or get in touch directly at darkexact@gmail.com or on social media at @darkexact. Thanks for being part of this project!

YOUR CARDS

THE AMULET

THE ANCHOR

THE ARROW

THE BELL

THE BLOOM

THE BOOT

THE BOUQUET

THE CANDLE

THE CHRYSALIS

THE CLOVER

THE COMPASS

THE CROWN

THE DAISY

THE DAGGER

THE EYE

THE FINCH

THE FOSSIL

THE FRUIT

THE GALAXY

THE HAND

THE HOURGLASS

THE KEY

THE LEAF

THE LENS

THE LIGHTNING

THE MOON

THE MOTH

THE PEACOCK

THE POPPY

THE RINGS

THE ROOT

THE SCYTHE

THE SEED

THE SHELL

THE SPELL

THE STAR

THE SUN

THE TREE

THE WINGS

ADDITIONAL NOTES

Made in the USA
Columbia, SC
26 October 2018